# A DK PUBLISHING BOOK

**Text** Terry Martin
**Project Editor** Caroline Bingham
**US Editor** Camela Decaire
**Senior Art Editor** Sarah Wright-Smith
**Deputy Managing Editor** Mary Ling
**Production** Louise Barratt
**Consultant** Theresa Greenaway
**Picture Researcher** Lorna Ainger
**Photography by** Paul Bricknell, Matthew Chattle,
Andreas Einsiedel, Steve Gorton, Peter Powell,
Susannah Price, Tim Ridley, Steve Shott

First American Edition, 1996
2 4 6 8 10 9 7 5 3

Published in the United States by DK Publishing, Inc.,
95 Madison Avenue, New York, New York 10016
http://www.dk.com
Copyright © 1996 Dorling Kindersley Limited, London

A CIP catalog record is available from the Library of Congress.

ISBN: 0-7894-1123-7

Color reproduction by Chromagraphics, Singapore
Printed and bound in Italy by L.E.G.O.

The publisher would like to thank the following for their
kind permission to reproduce their photographs: t top, b bottom,
l left, r right, c center, a above, BC back cover, FC front cover
Bruce Coleman Ltd.: Erwin & Peggy Bauer (Why does
the...?: c), Jane Burton (Why does it rain?: tr/Why do
dewdrops...?: c); Mr. Felix Labhardt FC cr, BC cr, Title page: bl,
(Why does it snow?: tr/ Why do dewdrops...?: tr), Dr. Scott Nielsen
FC tl, BC tl, (Why does it rain?: bc), Dr. Eckart Pott (Why is
ice...?: tr), John Shaw (Why do dewdrops...?: bl), Kim Taylor
FC bl, BC bl, Title page: tr, (Why does the...?: tl/Why is ice...?: tl,bl,
right-hand page: tl); Robert Harding Picture Library (Why is ice...?: c),
Fred Friberg (Why does it snow?: c); The Image Bank: Steve Dunwell
(Why is ice...?: c), Eric Meola (Why does the...?: tr), Pete Turner
(Why does lightning...?: bl); Frank Lane Picture Agency: R. Bird
(Why does lightning...?: br), W. Broadhurst (Why do
dewdrops...?: br), C. Carvalho (Why do rainbows...?: tr);
Photographer's Library: (Why is ice? right-hand page: br);
Pictor: Contents page: c, (Why is the...?: br/Why does it rain?:
tl,bl/Why does lightning...?: tr, Why does it snow?:
right-hand page: bl); Science Photo Library: John Mead
endpapers, Claude Nuridsany & Marie Perennou
FC cl, BC cl, Contents page: tc,ca, (Why does
it snow?: c); Tony Stone Images: (Why is the...?: c),
Beryl Bidwell (Why does it rain?: c), Bert Blokhuis (Why is the...?: tl), Val Corbett
(Why is ice...?: cl), George Hunter (Why do rainbows...?: bl), Richard Kaylin
(Why does lightning...?: c), Gary Yeowell BC c, (Why do rainbows...?: c).

# Questions

Why is the sun hot?

Why do rainbows appear?

Why does it rain?

Why does lightning strike?

Why does the wind blow?

Why does it snow?

Why is ice slippery?

Why do dewdrops appear overnight?

# WHY

## does lightning strike?

### Questions children ask about the weather

DK

# Why is the sun hot?

The sun is a burning ball of gases. We feel its heat, even though it's 93 million miles away. Hot stuff!

## Why can't I look at the sun?

The sun is much too bright for our delicate eyes and could cause blindness. It's rude to stare – and in this case, it's very dangerous.

The sun's heat brings changes in the weather.

**Why does it feel cold when a cloud covers the sun?**
Clouds soak up most of the sun's warm rays, just like a sponge soaks up water. The air near the ground soon cools – and this can spoil your fun in the sun.

# Why do rainbows

Rainbows appear when the sun's behind you and there's rain ahead because sunlight splits into colors as it passes through water droplets.

**Why are rainbows full of color?**
White sunlight is a perfect blend of seven colors: red, orange, yellow,

# appear?

**Why is this rainbow white?**
In the cold white Arctic, the sun creates the most amazing sights. This icebow forms when sunlight passes through falling ice crystals. These keep the sun's white rays together.

green, blue, indigo, and violet. So these are the colors that appear when a ray of sunlight passes through a raindrop and splits up.

# Why does it rain?

Clouds hold the answer. They carry tiny water droplets that bump into each other, growing bigger and heavier, until they fall, sprinkling or pouring, as rain.

### Why do clouds appear?
When warm air rises to meet cold air, moisture in the warm air condenses to make water droplets.

**Why are rain clouds so dark?**
Rain clouds appear dark because of the amount of water droplets inside them. The more droplets, the darker the cloud – and the harder it's going to rain!

These tiny droplets reflect sunlight, and a fluffy cloud appears.

# Why does lightning

A lightning bolt is a giant spark of electricity. It strikes because it is attracted to the ground in the same way that a magnet attracts certain metals.

**Why is thunder so noisy?**
The loud crashes of a heavy thunderstorm happen because scorching hot lightning makes air expand too fast. That makes a big boom.

# strike?

**Why does thunder follow lightning?**
Flash! Silence. Kaboom! Thunder and lightning occur at the same time, but sound travels much slower than light.

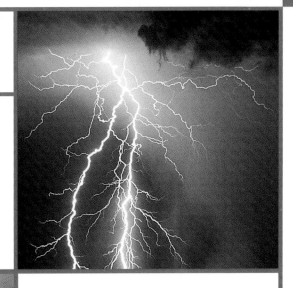

**Why shouldn't I stand under a tree for cover?**
When lightning strikes a tree, the electricity shoots down the trunk. It may electrocute you if you are too close.

# Why does the

Wind is whistling, invisible air. It blows because air never stops moving – warm air always rises, and cold air rushes in to take its place.

**Why do kites fly?**

Kites are made to fly "up, up, and away" on windy days. The stretched material is caught by the wind and pulled up. Hold the string tight!

# wind blow?

It's like a game of tag that never stops. It just gets faster or slower.

**Why do tornadoes appear?**
Tornadoes spiral up when a funnel of hot, damp air meets cold, dry air. They are dangerous whirlwinds, and they suck up everything in their path.

# Why does it snow?

Clouds can get so cold their water droplets freeze into tiny ice crystals. The crystals cling to each other as they fall from the sky, turning into soft snowflakes.

**Why is a snowflake star shaped?**
It isn't! It's made up of about 50 tiny crystals that are. Each crystal has six sides, and no two are the same. You can only see the crystals through a microscope.

**Why does a snowman take so long to melt?** Snow reflects the sun's heat and light away, and when it is squashed tightly together, as in a snowman's body, it can even refreeze when temperatures drop overnight!

# Why is ice slippery?

When skating across ice, your weight melts the top layer, creating a slippery surface between your skates and the ice.

**Why do leaves get frosty?**

Water in the air can freeze on a cold, solid surface – such as a leaf or window. It is known as hoar frost.

## Why do icicles appear?

Spikes of ice slowly grow when drops of water freeze before they can drip to the ground.

## Why are icebergs so big?

An iceberg is a broken-off piece of glacier that floats in the sea. The floating crystal castle you see is just the tip of the iceberg. The rest of it is hidden under the water.

# Why do dewdrops appear

As air cools at night, the moisture it contains condenses into droplets.
By morning, these droplets are clinging to all sorts of things, from spiders' webs to insects' wings.

**Why do we have mist?**
Just like dew, mist appears when water in the air condenses into

# overnight?

**Why is fog thick?**
Fog is thicker than mist because it contains many more water droplets. In cities these can pick up dirt from cars and smoke.

droplets. This makes a cloud appear – but it appears at ground level, so you can walk through it!